The Arachnid Class

Family Trees

The Arachnid Class

REBECCA STEFOFF

Marshall Cavendish
Benchmark
New York

Marshall Cavendish Benchmark
99 White Plains Road
Tarrytown, New York 10591
www.marshallcavendish.us
Text copyright © 2009 by Rebecca Stefoff
Illustrations copyright © 2009 by Marshall Cavendish Corporation
Illustrations by Robert Romagnoli

All Web sites were available and accurate when this book was sent to press.

Editor: Karen Ang
Publisher: Michelle Bisson
Art Director: Anahid Hamparian
Series Designer: Patrice Sheridan

Library of Congress Cataloging-in-Publication Data
Stefoff, Rebecca, date
The arachnid class / by Rebecca Stefoff.
p. cm. -- (Family trees)
Includes bibliographical references and index.
Summary: "Explores the habitats, life cycles, and other characteristics of arachnids, such as spiders, scorpions, mites, and ticks"--Provided by publisher.
ISBN 978-0-7614-3075-9
1. Arachnida--Juvenile literature. I. Title. II. Series.

QL452.2.S74 2008
595.4--dc22
2008017561

Front cover: A crab spider
Title page: A scorpion
Back cover: A scorpion

Photo Research by Candlepants Incorporated
Cover Photo: age fotostock / Super Stock

The photographs in this book are used by permission and through the courtesy of:
Shutterstock: 3, 7, 11(both), 13, 19, 27, 30, 31, 33, 35, 37, 53, 41, 48, 51, 54, 76, 82, 83. Minden Pictures: Piotr Naskrecki, 6, 44, 57, 61, 62, 64, 77; Mark Moffett, 26, 36; Gerry Ellis, 32; Stephen Dalton, 38, 43, 56; Michael and Patricia Fogden, 45; Kim Taylor / npl, 52; Heidi and Hans-Jurgen Koch, 67; Claus Meyer, 81. Corbis: Hulton-Deutsch Collection, 9; Jonathan Blair, 18; Colin Keates, 21; Layne Kennedy, 23; Esther Beaton, 39; Visuals Unlimited, 72, 73, 78; Joe McDonald, 80; Frans Lemmens / zefa, back cover. Alamy Images: Phil Degginger, 20; fotototo, 29; blickwinkel, 34, 40, 65; Alasdair Thomson, 42; Florida Images, 47; cbimages, 49; Chris Mattison, 50; Phototake Inc., 68, 70; WildPictures, 69. Animals_Animals: M. Fogden/OSF, 59. Super Stock: age fotostock, 74, 84. AP Images: USFWS, Gordon Smith, 87.

Printed in Malaysia
1 3 5 6 4 2

CONTENTS

INTRODUCTION	Classifying Life	7
	Animal Kingdom Family Tree	16
CHAPTER ONE	Arachnid Basics	19
CHAPTER TWO	The Spiders	33
CHAPTER THREE	From Scorpions to Dust Mites	53
CHAPTER FOUR	The Lives of Arachnids	75
Glossary		88
Arachnid Family Tree		90
Find Out More		92
Bibliography		94
Index		95

Gasteracantha cancriformis, usually called a crab spider or spiny-backed orb weaver, lives in Florida and other warm parts of the western hemisphere. It occurs in red, yellow, orange, and white forms. The spines may protect the spider from predators or disguise it as a thorny blossom.

Classifying Life

According to the ancient Greeks and Romans, a young woman named Arachne wove the most beautiful cloth anyone had ever seen. Arachne was proud of her weaving ability—a little too proud. After Arachne boasted that she was a better weaver than Athena, the goddess of weaving (among other things), the girl ended up in a weaving contest with the goddess.

Each of them wove a tapestry, a wall hanging with a picture in colored thread. Athena's tapestry showed a glorious victory she had won over the sea god, Poseidon. Arachne's tapestry highlighted some of the gods' less glorious moments, such as Zeus, the king of the gods, cheating on his wife. Although Athena admitted that Arachne had marvelous skill, she could not overlook Arachne's mockery. The goddess destroyed Arachne's tapesty and the loom on which she had woven it. Overcome with shame, Arachne rushed off to hang herself. Athena showed mercy and let Arachne live—but the goddess turned the girl into a spider who would spend eternity weaving.

Arachne's name is the Greek word for "spider." It is also the source of the scientific term "arachnid." Spiders, however, are not the only arachnids. The term also applies to scorpions, mites, ticks, and other creatures that are less well-known, such as vinegaroons and harvestmen. To understand how these arachnids are related to each other, and how they fit into the natural world, it helps to know something about how scientists classify living things.

THE INVENTION OF TAXONOMY

Science gives us tools for making sense of the natural world. One of the most powerful tools is classification, which means organizing things in a pattern according to their differences and similarities. Since ancient times, scientists who study living things have been developing a classification system for living things. This system is called taxonomy. Scientists use taxonomy to group together organisms that share features, setting them apart from other organisms with different features.

Taxonomy is hierarchical, which means that it is arranged in levels. The highest levels are categories that include many kinds of organisms. These large categories are divided into smaller categories, which in turn are divided into still smaller ones. The most basic category is the species, a single kind of organism.

The idea behind taxonomy is simple, but the world of living things is complex and full of surprises. Taxonomy is not a fixed pattern. It keeps changing to reflect new knowledge or ideas. Over time, scientists have developed rules for adjusting the pattern even when they disagree on the details.

One of the first taxonomists was the ancient Greek philosopher Aristotle (384-322 BCE), who investigated many branches of science, including biology. Aristotle arranged living things on a sort of ladder, or scale. At the bottom were those he considered lowest, or least developed, such as worms. Above them were things he considered higher, or more developed, such as fish, then birds, then mammals.

For centuries after Aristotle, taxonomy made little progress. People who studied nature tended to group organisms together by features that

Tropical plants and animals fascinated European scientists of the nineteenth century. A German book from that period shows a guava plant with a variety of tropical spiders devouring flies, ants, and even a hummingbird.

were easy to see, such as separating trees from grasses or birds from fish. However, they did not try to develop a system for classifying all life. Then, between 1682 and 1705, an English naturalist named John Ray published a plan of the living world that was designed to have a place for every species of plant and animal. Ray's system was hierarchical, with several levels of larger and smaller categories. It was the foundation of modern taxonomy.

Swedish naturalist Carolus Linnaeus (1707-1778) built on that foundation to create the taxonomic system used today. Linnaeus was chiefly interested in plants, but his system of classification included all living things. Its highest level of classification was the kingdom. To Linnaeus, everything belonged to either the plant kingdom or the animal kingdom. Each of these kingdoms was divided into a number of smaller categories called classes. Each class was divided into orders. Each order was divided into genera. Each genus (the singular form of genera) contained one or more species.

Linnaeus also developed another of Ray's ideas, a method for naming species. Before Linnaeus published his important work *System of Nature* in 1735, scientists had no recognized system for referring to plants and animals. Organisms were generally known by their common names, but many of them had different names in various countries. Two naturalists might call the same plant or animal by two different names—or use the same name for two different organisms.

To end the confusion, so that scholars everywhere could communicate clearly about plants and animals, Linnaeus started the practice of giving each plant or animal a two-part scientific name made up of its genus and species. These names were in Latin, the scientific language of Linnaeus's day. For example, the Tasmanian funnel-web spider's scientific name is *Hadronyche venenata* (or *H. venenata* after the first time the full name is used). The genus *Hadronyche* contains a dozen or so species of funnel-web spiders that live in eastern Australia. The Tasmanian funnel-web spider is set apart from the other species in the genus by the second part of its name, *venenata.*

Linnaeus named hundreds of species. Other scientists quickly adopted his highly flexible system to name many more. The Linnaean system appeared at a time when European naturalists were exploring the rest of the world and finding thousands of new plants and animals. This flood of discoveries was overwhelming at times, but Linnaean taxonomy helped scientists identify and organize their finds.

TAXONOMY TODAY

Biologists still use the system of scientific naming that Linnaeus developed. Anyone who discovers a new species can choose its scientific name, which is usually in Latin, or once in a while in Greek. Other aspects of taxonomy, though, have changed since Linnaeus's time.

Over the years, as biologists learned more about the similarities and differences among living things, they added new levels to taxonomy.

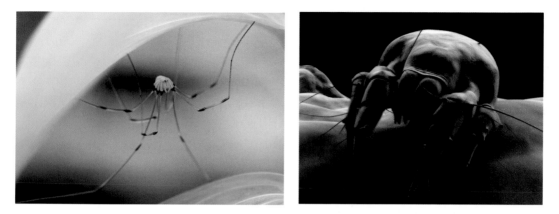

The harvestman picking its way along a leaf (left) and the mite magnified by an electron microscope (right) share the defining features of the arachnid class, including eight segmented legs.

Eventually, an organism's full classification could include the following taxonomic levels: kingdom, subkingdom, phylum (some biologists use division instead of phylum for plants and fungi), subphylum, superclass, class, subclass, infraclass, order, superfamily, family, genus, species, and subspecies or variety.

Another change concerned the kinds of information that scientists use to classify organisms. The earliest naturalists used obvious physical features, such as the differences between fish and birds, to divide organisms into groups. By the time of Ray and Linnaeus, naturalists could study specimens in more detail. Aided by new tools such as the microscope, they explored the inner structures of plants and animals. For a long time after Linnaeus, classification was based mainly on details of anatomy, or physical structure, although scientists also looked at how an organism reproduced and how and where it lived.

Today, biologists can peer more deeply into an organism's inner workings than Aristotle or Linnaeus ever dreamed possible. They can look inside its individual cells and study the arrangement of DNA that makes up its genetic blueprint. Genetic information is key to modern classification because DNA is more than an organism's blueprint. DNA also reveals

11

how closely the organism is related to other species and how long ago those species separated during the process of evolution.

In recent years, many biologists have pointed out that the Linnaean system is a patchwork of old and new ideas. It doesn't clearly reflect the latest knowledge about the evolutionary links among organisms both living and extinct. Some scientists now call for a new approach to taxonomy, one that is based entirely on evolutionary relationships. One of the most useful new approaches is called phylogenetics, the study of organisms' evolutionary histories. In this approach, scientists group together all organisms that are descended from the same ancestor. The result is branching, treelike diagrams called cladograms. These cladograms show the order in which groups of plants or animals split off from their shared ancestors.

None of the proposed new systems of classifying living things has been accepted by all scientists, but the move toward a phylogenetic approach is under way. Still, scientists continue to use the two main features of Linnaean taxonomy: the hierarchy of categories and the two-part species name. Experts may disagree about the proper term for a category, however, or about how to classify a particular plant or animal. Because scientists create and use classifications for many different purposes, there is no single "right" way to classify organisms.

Even at the highest level of classification, scientists take different approaches to taxonomy. A few of them still divide all life into two kingdoms, plants and animals. At the other extreme are scientists who divide life into thirteen or more kingdoms, possibly grouping the kingdoms into larger categories called domains or superkingdoms. Most scientists, though, use classification systems with five to seven kingdoms: plants, animals, fungi, and several kingdoms of microscopic organisms such as bacteria, amoebas, and algae.

The classification of living things is always changing, as scientists learn more about the connections among organisms. Early taxonomists, for example, grouped the spiders with the insects. Insects and spiders do share several features, such as jointed legs and bodies covered with outer casings called exoskeletons, which take the place of internal skeletons. Other creatures, such as crabs, also have these features. Eventually scientists grouped insects, spiders, crabs, and other joint-legged, exoskeletal animals together in a phylum called the arthropods. Recognizing many differences between insects and spiders, they placed insects in one class within the arthropod phylum. Spiders and their close relatives got their own class, the Arachnida.

Today scientists have divided arachnids into a number of different orders: one order for spiders, one for scorpions, and so on. The number of orders in the arachnid class may vary slightly from one taxonomist to the next, but many experts use a system with eleven arachnid orders. Some of

Since ancient times people have admired the spider's ability to weave intricate patterns of silken threads. Modern scientists have discovered that, for its weight, spider silk is as strong as steel.

Classifying the Black Widow Spider

More than thirty kinds of widow spiders are found around the world. They contain a venom called a neurotoxin, which attacks the nervous system of their prey. (The bite of a black widow spider usually just makes a human adult sick, but once in a while it is fatal.) The widow spiders' name comes from the fact that the females sometimes become "widows" by killing and eating their partners after mating. The term "black widow" is often used for the three species of North American widow spiders—the northern, southern, and western black widows. Here is the scientific classification of the western black widow spider, *Latrodectus hesperus:*

Kingdom	Animalia (animals)
Phylum	Athropoda (animals with jointed limbs and outer coverings called exoskeletons in place of internal skeletons; includes insects, crustaceans, arachnids, and others)
Subphylum	Chelicerata (arthropods with a pair of pointed appendages for grasping food; includes arachnids, horseshoe crabs, and sea spiders)
Class	Arachnida (eleven orders of arachnids)
Order	Araneae (more than 110 families of spiders)
Family	Theridiidae (more than 2,200 species of tangle-web spiders)
Genus	*Lactrodectus* (more than 30 species of widow spiders worldwide)
Species	*Hesperus* (western black widow spider)

these orders, such as the spiders, are fairly well known to both scientists and the general public. Others, such as the microwhip scorpions and the hooded tick spiders, are much less familiar. Arachnologist Mark S. Harvey has called these smaller orders the "neglected cousins" of the arachnid class.

From spiders that devour mosquitoes by the millions to soil mites that help recycle dead plants and animals, arachnids fill vital roles in the world's ecosystems. They also inspire emotions ranging from admiration to arachnaphobia, which is fear and loathing of arachnids, particularly spiders. Although people have studied spiders and their kin since ancient times, much remains to be learned about this large and varied class of creatures. Arachnologists, the scientists who specialize in studying spiders and other arachnids, estimate the number of known arachnid species at more than 80,000. And thousands of arachnid species, they agree, remain to be discovered and studied by future arachnologists.

Scientists classify living things in arrangements like this family tree of the animal

ANIMAL

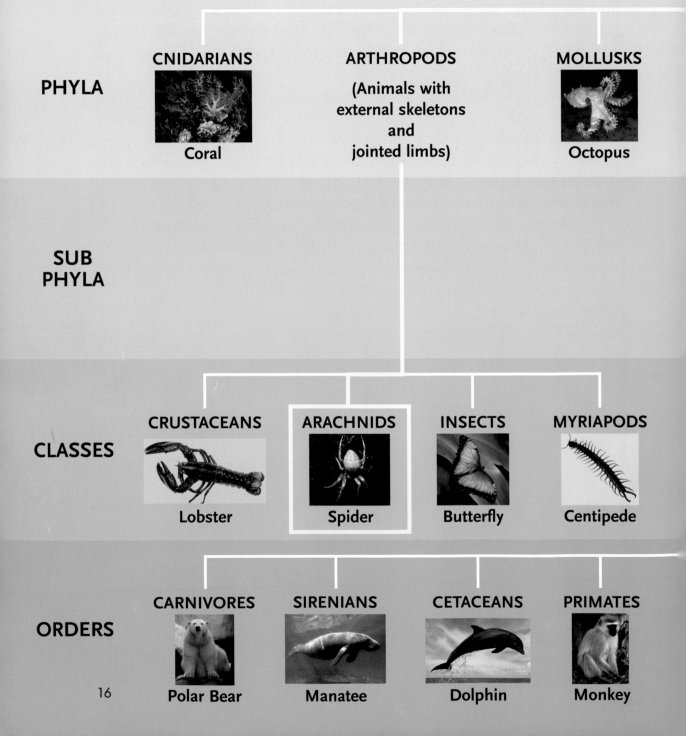

PHYLA

CNIDARIANS
Coral

ARTHROPODS
(Animals with external skeletons and jointed limbs)

MOLLUSKS
Octopus

SUB PHYLA

CLASSES

CRUSTACEANS
Lobster

ARACHNIDS
Spider

INSECTS
Butterfly

MYRIAPODS
Centipede

ORDERS

CARNIVORES
Polar Bear

SIRENIANS
Manatee

CETACEANS
Dolphin

PRIMATES
Monkey

16

kingdom to highlight the connections and the differences among the many forms of life.

KINGDOM

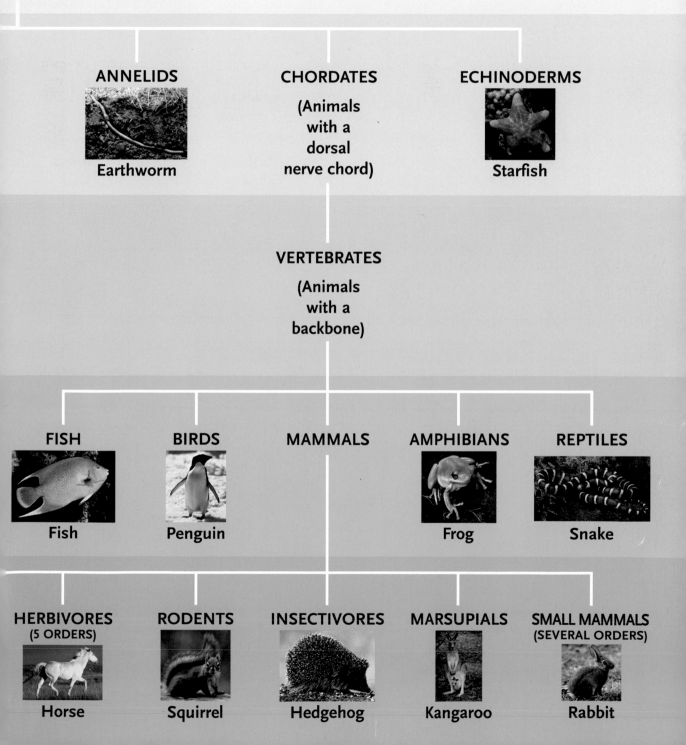

ANNELIDS

Earthworm

CHORDATES

(Animals with a dorsal nerve chord)

ECHINODERMS

Starfish

VERTEBRATES

(Animals with a backbone)

FISH

Fish

BIRDS

Penguin

MAMMALS

AMPHIBIANS

Frog

REPTILES

Snake

HERBIVORES
(5 ORDERS)

Horse

RODENTS

Squirrel

INSECTIVORES

Hedgehog

MARSUPIALS

Kangaroo

SMALL MAMMALS
(SEVERAL ORDERS)

Rabbit

The 49-million-year-old spider in this German fossil was a male orb weaver. It was very similar to arachnid species still in existence.

Arachnid Basics

Arachnids come in an amazing variety of shapes and sizes. All of them, however, share the same basic body plan and biology. Arachnids inherited these features from distant ancestors that were some of the first creatures to leave the ancient seas for life on land hundreds of millions of years ago.

EXPLOSIVE ORIGINS

Paleontologists, the scientists who study the fossil remains of ancient and extinct life forms, take special interest in a period they call the Cambrian explosion. During this period, which began about 545 million years ago and lasted until about 530 million years ago, life on earth "exploded" into many new forms. The earliest ancestors of most life forms that exist today appeared during that Cambrian explosion.

All Cambrian life was aquatic, or water-dwelling. The oceans were home to a number of soft-bodied, mostly small types of animals. Over the Cambrian period, some of them evolved into the first recognizable forms of animals known today. Among these new forms were sponges, worms, snails, and chordates—fish with spinal cords, creatures that would eventually give rise to all animals that have skeletons, including mammals. Another life form that appeared during the Cambrian explosion was the arthropod, an animal with its skeleton on the outside.

Arthropods had limbs that bent at one or more joints. Their bodies and limbs were covered with exoskeletons. These tough outer casings cannot stretch, so in order to increase in size, every so often arthropods had to molt, or shed their exoskeletons. This left the creatures soft and vulnerable until the newly exposed exoskeleton hardened.

Five main groups of arthropods evolved in Cambrian times. The trilobites later became extinct, but the other four groups still exist. They are the myriapods (creatures with many legs, such as centipedes and

A fossil from Morocco's Sahara Desert is of an ocean-dwelling creature called a trilobite, an early kind of arthropod that became extinct long ago. Around 520 million years ago, when this trilobite lived, the land that is now northern Africa was covered by a sea.

With a segmented body and long tail, this fossilized creature resembles a modern scorpion. It belonged to an extinct group of aquatic arthropods called the eurypterids, or sea scorpions.

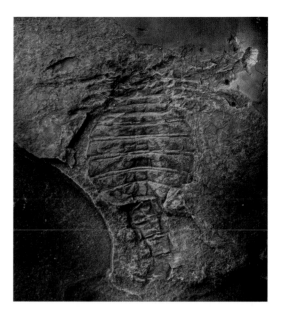

millipedes), the insects (creatures with six legs), the crustaceans (hard-shelled, mostly aquatic creatures such as crabs and shrimp), and the chelicerates. Unlike other arthropods, chelicerates do not have antennae. A chelicerate's key feature is its mouthparts. Instead of jaws, chelicerates have a pair of short, pointed fangs called chelicerae at the front of their bodies. They use their chelicerae to grip and bite their prey.

The first chelicerates, like all early life forms, lived in the sea. Three groups of them stayed there. The eurypterids, also called sea scorpions, became extinct. The other two kinds of aquatic chelicerates still exist. They are the horseshoe crabs and the pycnogonids, or sea spiders. A fourth group of chelicerates migrated onto land sometime after 500 million years ago. This group became the arachnids.

The oldest known arachnid fossil, dating from about 410 million years ago, is a scorpion, and many scientists think that scorpions were the first arachnids. Some early scorpion fossils have gills, organs that animals use to absorb oxygen from water. Gills are one sign that scorpions started out as aquatic animals. Another sign is size. *Prearcturus gigas* and *Gigantoscorpio willsi* are scorpions that lived between 350 and 390 million years ago. Scientists know from their fossils that these species were much larger than any scorpion alive today. Measuring about 3 feet (1 meter) long, these ancient scorpions could only have lived in water, at least while molting—their legs would have been too soft to support their weight on land.

As early as 400 million years ago, however, some scorpion species spent their entire lives on land. Other types of terrestrial, or land-dwelling, arthropods appear in the fossil record at about the same time. In 2001 paleontologists working in Scotland found fossils of a 400-million-year-old harvestman, a type of arachnid that still exists today. The earliest spider fossils are almost that old. One of them, *Attercopus fimbriungus,* dates from 380 million years ago.

Over time, spiders evolved new features. In early spiders, the chelicerae or fangs moved straight down when the spider pinned its prey. By about 250 million years ago, some spiders had evolved chelicerae that moved toward the center from each side. These spiders could grasp their prey by closing their fangs inward. Another important development was the ability to spin silk from special glands called spinnerets. Fossils show that spiders had evolved spinnerets by around 250 million years ago. At first they probably used their silk to make draglines, strands that supported their weight and acted as safety lines when they climbed. By about 160 million years ago, however, some spiders were spinning the elaborate, spiral-patterned webs made by modern orb weaver spiders.

Some of the best-preserved ancient spiders and other arachnids are not fossils in stone. They are bodies found inside pieces of amber, a hard, clear yellow or brown substance formed when the resin of certain trees hardens over long periods of time. Small creatures that happened to get stuck in fresh resin millions of years ago have been preserved in amber until modern times. A few choice pieces of amber more than 100 million years old contain spiders with their prey, or with pieces of their webs.

As time passed, many kinds of early arachnids became extinct. Others continued to evolve, but although they acquired new features, their overall appearance did not greatly change. Today's scorpions, spiders, and other arachnids are similar in many ways to their ancient ancestors. Basic

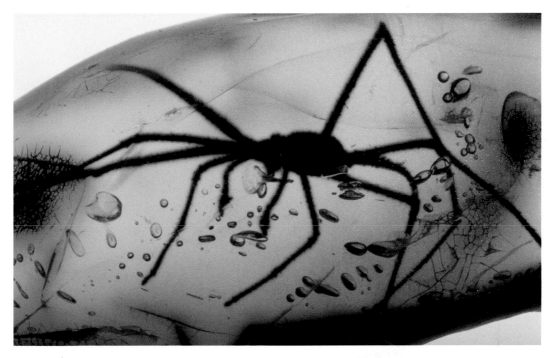

Amber, long prized as a gem, is golden-brown tree resin that has fossilized and become as hard as stone. This spider may have ventured into fresh-flowing, sticky resin in pursuit of insect prey. Trapped, the spider was covered and preserved for millions of years.

arachnid structure and biology have proved highly successful, helping this large group of animals survive for hundreds of millions of years.

THE ARACHNID BODY PLAN

An arachnid consists of a central body and six pairs of appendages, or limbs. The body of an arachnid has two parts. The front part is the cephalothorax, also called the prosoma. The rear half is the abdomen, or opisthosoma.

In many kinds of arachnids, including most spiders, it is easy to identify the cephalothorax and the abdomen. The two parts are joined at a

The Biggest Spider That Ever Lived

A 300-million-year-old fossil found in the South American nation of Argentina in 1980 became famous as "the biggest spider that ever lived." With a 1.6-foot-long (.5-meter-long) body and a legspan of 20 inches (50 centimeters), this extinct creature was compared in size to a dog. It was given the name *Megarachne*, meaning "giant spider." For twenty-five years, while the fossil's owners stored it in a bank vault, museum-goers around the world shuddered at models of *Megarachne*. The spider even appeared in the *Guinness Book of Records* as the world's largest spider.

In 2005, a British arachnologist named Paul Selden gained permission to examine the *Megarachne* fossil. He discovered that it wasn't a spider after all. Selden thinks that *Megarachne* was a eurypterid, a member of an extinct group of sea scorpions. Scientists hope to study the fossil further, or to find more *Megarachne* fossils, but experts no longer regard *Megarachne* as a spider. Most of them agree that the biggest spider known to science is a species that is alive today in the forests of northern South America: *Theraphosa leblondi*, the Goliath bird-eating spider. This member of the tarantula family can have a body almost 5 inches (13 cm) long, with a legspan of 10 inches (25 cm)—making it about the size of a small chihuahua.

narrow seam, called the waist. In other arachnids, however, there is no waist. The front and rear parts of the bodies seem to be joined in a single section. Many ticks and mites, for example, are round or oval, with no clearly defined cephalothorax or abdomen. Inside their bodies, however, these arachnids are divided into two parts, even if the division is not visible from the outside.

EXTERNAL ANATOMY OF A SPIDER

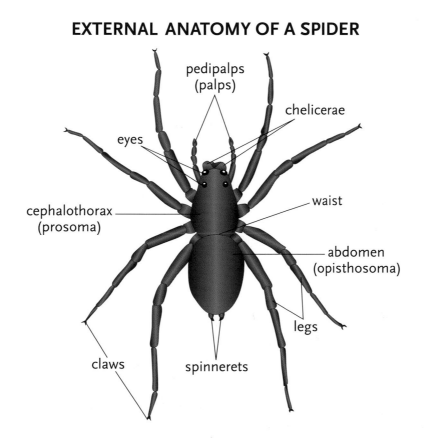

pedipalps
(palps)

chelicerae

eyes

cephalothorax
(prosoma)

waist

abdomen
(opisthosoma)

legs

claws

spinnerets

All of an arachnid's appendages are attached to its cephalothorax. There are twelve appendages in all, with half of each pair—or six appendages—on each side of the cephalothorax. The first pair of appendages is the chelicerae, the short pincers or fangs that the arachnid uses in feeding. These hang down in front of the arachnid's mouth opening.

The second pair of appendages is the pedipalps, sometimes called palps. These have different uses in different groups of arachnids. Some arachnids use their palps as an extra pair of legs. Some have palps that take the form of claws or pincers for seizing and crushing prey. Males of many species use their palps in reproduction, to pass sperm to the females.

Four pairs of walking legs form the arachnid's remaining appendages. Each leg ends in two or three tiny claws. These help arachnids keep their grip while walking or running over steep or uneven surfaces. Two orders of arachnids, called whip spiders and whip scorpions, use just three pairs of legs for walking. In these arachnids, the first pair of legs has evolved into long, whiplike appendages that the animals use as feelers to help them "see" their surroundings. The whip spiders and whip scorpions have turned two of their eight legs into a pair of sense organs that are similar to antennae.

The arachnid's body and legs are contained within a casing called an exoskeleton or cuticle. It is made of a durable, stiff, waterproof material called chitin. The exoskeleton acts as both the arachnid's skeleton and its skin. It supports the animal's organs and muscles, and it protects the internal organs from the environment. Some arachnids have an extra-thick plate

The leg of a West African tarantula ends in a rounded bulb called a tarsal pad, equipped with claws. All spiders have claws, although the claws are not easy to see on smaller spiders.

An amblypygid or whip spider uses the first pair of its legs not for walking but for sensing its surroundings. As it moves, it feels its way with these long legs, which have a whiplike appearance.

or shield of chitin, called a carapace, on their "backs"—the upper surface of the cephalothorax.

ARACHNID ORGANS AND SENSES

Like all animals, arachnids must breathe to live. Within the arachnid class, animals have three ways of breathing. Extremely small arachnids, such as some mites, simply absorb oxygen from the air through tiny openings in their exoskeletons, and the oxygen spreads through their systems.

Most arachnids, however, have specialized organs for drawing air into their systems. They have book lungs, or tracheae, or both. Book lungs

INTERNAL ANATOMY OF A SPIDER

intestine　　heart　　digestive gland

pumping stomach

brain

eye

excretory tubules

ovary

anus

spinnerets　　trachea

spiracle

book lung

gut

mouth

poison gland

are membranes, or thin layers of blood-filled tissue, stacked like the pages of a book. Tracheae are tubes lined with similar membranes. Air enters the lungs or tracheae through spiracles, openings in the exoskeleton. From the spiracles the air travels across the membranes of the lungs or tracheae. As air circulates around the membranes, oxygen passes from the air through the membranes into the arachnid's blood. At the same time, waste gases such as carbon dioxide pass from the blood out into the air.

Arachnid blood is called hemolymph. Although arachnids have hearts and blood vessels to pump hemolymph to all parts of the body, the hemolymph is not found only in the blood vessels. It fills the inside of the arachnid's body, washing around all the organs. The hemolymph contains a copper compound that carries oxygen. This copper gives hemolymph a blue color.

Nearly all arachnids are carnivores, or meat-eaters, although some mites and harvestmen eat vegetable matter. But whether they are carnivores or herbivores, arachnids cannot eat solid food. They must turn their food into liquid that they can suck up.

Like all arachnids, ticks require liquid food. Here the food is blood drawn from a human host. This tick species, *Ixodes ricinus,* can spread disease among sheep and humans.

To feed, an arachnid seizes its prey with its pedipalps and injects it with venom from its chelicerae. The arachnid then coats or fills the prey with digestive juices that leave the arachnid's body through special openings in the chelicerae. These digestive juices start turning the prey into soup. Once the food has been liquefied, the arachnid draws it in with pumping or sucking actions of its stomach.

Arachnids are aware of the world around them through a number of senses, some of which scientists do not yet fully understand. Sensory equipment varies from one kind of arachnid to another. A few species of cave-dwelling arachnids are eyeless, but most arachnids have at least two eyes. Many types have four, six, or eight eyes. A jumping spider, for example, may have either two or four large eyes as well as four small eyes.

Its four large and four smaller eyes give this adult wolf spider better eyesight than most other kinds of arachnids. Wolf spiders are hunters that rely on their eyesight to spot and run down their prey.

Arachnid eyes may be set either in the front of the cephalothorax or along the sides.

Arachnids also have chemical senses, although scientists are not sure how these senses work. Experts do know that arachnids can detect certain chemicals, such as pheromones, or substances given off by possible mating partners. Some arachnologists think that arachnids may smell or taste substances through their tarsal pits, which are small organs on their legs that are sensitive to moisture and temperature. Others think that arachnids have scent organs that are not yet known.

Vibration is an extremely important dimension of an arachnid's world. Most arachnids can sense vibrations in the ground through their legs. In addition, many arachnids have hairy bodies. Those that are not hairy often have at least a few hairs, or possibly spines or stiff bristles called setae, on their bodies and appendages. These hairs, spines, and bristles have important sensory functions. When the arachnid touches something, or something touches the arachnid, the hairs or bristles detect pressure. They can also feel air currents caused by something moving nearby.

The pattern on the abdomen of *Aranea gemmoides* has earned this arachnid the names catface and monkeyface spider. Hairs and bristles on an archnid's body and legs are important sensory organs that help the creature gather information about its surroundings and possible prey.

Each arachnid's particular combination of senses allows it to detect prey, danger, and potential mates or rivals. The arachnid knows its world very well, even if that world is as small as the underside of a log, or a web in the corner of a room.

Large and active, hunting spiders are commonly found in forests and fields, although they occasionally make their way indoors. Some people welcome spiders into their homes because the arachnids kill pests such as cockroaches and flies.

The Spiders

Spiders are everywhere. They live in deserts, tropical rain forests, and almost every other kind of natural environment. Mountain climbers have found spiders living among rocks and ice at altitudes as high as 22,000 feet (6,666 m) on Mt. Everest and other towering peaks. One species, the European water spider, *Argyroneta aquatica,* has even evolved the ability to live underwater in ponds and streams, where it preys on tiny minnows and other aquatic creatures. The water spider carries bubbles of air into the water in the hairs on its legs, then stores the air in its underwater lair, a dome or bell made of spider silk.

Spiders are numerous as well as adaptable. Most human environments, such as houses and office buildings, are home to hundreds or even thousands of spiders that are never seen by the people who live and work there. Some outdoor settings can support enormous numbers of spiders. In the 1940s, for example, a British arachnologist named S.W. Bristowe calculated, based on years of studying spiders in England, that an acre of grassy meadowland could contain as many as 2.25 million spiders.

For most people around the world, spiders are the most familiar arachnids. They also make up one of the best-studied orders in the

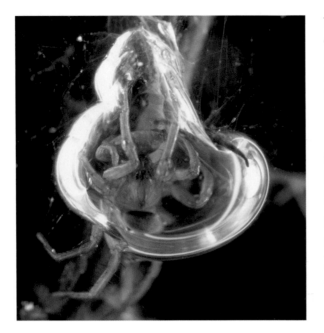

The European water spider is the only arachnid that spends its entire life in water, breathing air that it pulls beneath the surface in tiny bubbles and then stores in a tank, or air bell, made of silk.

arachnid class. Scientists have identified more than 110 families and 40,000 or so species of spiders. They group these into three suborders: the mesothelids, the mygalomorphs, and the araneomorphs.

MESOTHELIDS: LIVING FOSSILS

The rare and seldom-seen mesothelid spiders are survivors of a very ancient branch of the spider family. Arachnologists call the mesothelids primitive or basal spiders, which means that they have some ancestral features—features seen in fossils of the earliest known spiders. Mesothelids are sometimes considered living fossils among the spiders, because they have survived with very little change for more than 200 million years.

The mesothelid spider's most distinctive feature is its abdomen, which is divided into sections, or segments, that can easily be seen. Mesothelid spiders also have sections of carapace on their cephalothoraxes and abdomens, giving them an armor-plated appearance. All mesothelids have four pairs of spinnerets. These are located on the bottom of the abdomen, not at the rear of the body as in more modern spiders. Another distinctive feature is that mesothelids do not have venom glands. All other spiders, except for two small families, have venom glands.

About 90 species of mesothelid spiders are known to exist today. They are found only in caves and forested regions in Southeast Asia, southeastern China, or southern Japan. Mesothelids live in burrows or holes that are lined with silk and covered by trapdoors. Most species leave strands of silk, called fishing lines, trailing from the mouths of their burrows. If an insect or other prey touches one of the these lines, the trapdoor flips open and the spider rushes out to grab the passing meal.

MYGALOMORPHS: TARANTULAS AND THEIR RELATIVES

The mygalomorph suborder of spiders contains about fifteen families. Among them are the largest spiders in the world, and the most dangerous to humans.

The most distinctive feature of the mygalomorph spiders is their chelicerae, or fangs. The fangs move straight up and down in a stabbing motion. (The mygalomorphs share this feature with the mesothelid spiders, but mygalomorphs do not have segmented abdomens like the mesothelids.)

The best-known mygalomorphs are the tarantulas. In strict scientific terms, the only true tarantulas are about 900 or so members of a single

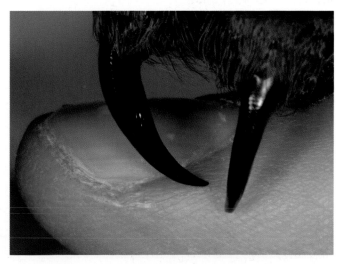

A tarantula's fangs can pierce human skin. Tarantulas are mygalomorph spiders, which means that their fangs stab downward to impale their prey.

: family, *Theraphosidae*. These large, hairy spiders are found in Australia, southern Asia (where they may be known as bird spiders), Africa (where they are often called baboon spiders), South America, and the southern parts of North America and Europe. The name "tarantula," however, has often been applied to other large spiders, such as wolf spiders and funnel-web spiders.

Some tarantulas are terrestrial. Others are arboreal, or tree-dwelling. They build tentlike webs in the branches, and there they live and hunt. All tarantulas are venomous, but although some of their bites can be quite painful to humans, none is known to be fatal. Most serious problems with tarantula bites happen when the bite becomes infected or when a person has an allergic reaction to one or more chemicals in the venom.

Some tarantula species in the Americas have a defensive weapon called urticating hairs. When threatened, the tarantula rubs its legs against a patch of these stiff hairs on its abdomen, making the hairs fly toward the enemy. If the hairs land in the eyes, nose, or mouth of a bird or animal that wants to eat the tarantula, they cause such intense discomfort that the predator may retreat, leaving the spider alone.

Many experts consider *Theraphosa blondi,* the goliath or bird-eating spider of South America, to be the world's largest spider. This tarantula has been known to kill birds, mice, and lizards, as well as other spiders.

A tarantula leaves its burrow near Napo, in the South American nation of Ecuador.

In addition to tarantulas, the mygalomorph suborder includes the Dipluridae, or funnel-web spiders. These spiders have flat bodies. Carapaces on their cephalothoraxes may have a waxy or leathery appearance. A few members of this group live in Europe and North America, but most are found in the tropics. Funnel-web spiders weave dense, sheetlike webs. Set in the web is a tube that has a wide mouth but becomes narrow as it gets deeper, like a funnel. Inside this funnel the spider waits for prey to become entangled in the web. The funnel-web spider's typical prey is insects or other small arthropods such as centipedes, but, as with tarantulas, large species sometimes prey on small lizards or birds.

The most dangerous member of the funnel-web family is an Australian species called *Atrax robustus*, the Sydney funnel-web spider.

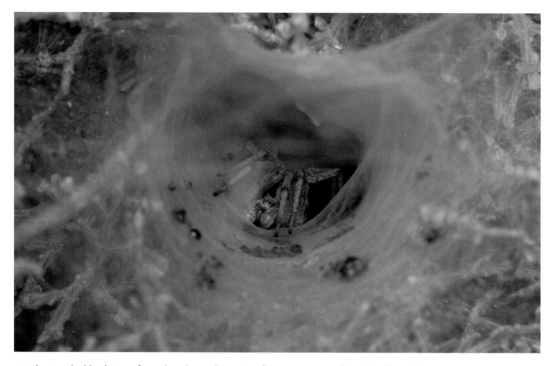

Inside its tubelike lair, a funnel-web spider waits for prey to stumble into the web.

Males of this species have bodies about 1.5 inch (4 cm) long. They also have aggressive tempers, especially when they are moving around looking for mates. These spiders are likely to bite anything that moves near them, and their venom, which contains a powerful poison called atraxotoxin, is extremely strong. Before scientists developed an antidote in 1981, the bite of *A. robustus* is known to have killed more than a dozen people. Some earlier deaths may have been caused by this spider's bite, too. Arachnologists consider the Sydney funnel-web to be the deadliest spider in the world.

Trap-door spiders are found in many parts of the world. These mygalomorph spiders belong to the family Ctenizidae. They are excellent tunnelers that dig with their fangs. Along each edge of a trap-door spider's

The Sydney funnel-web spider's bite was deadly before scientists developed a treatment. Australians have learned to beware of this arachnid, which can be found in brush and gardens.

fang is a structure called a rastellum, a set of strong spines, which helps the spider cut through the earth.

Depending on the size of the species, a trap-door spider's burrow ranges in length from just an inch or two (2.5 to 5 cm) to several feet (more than .5 m). Some of the bigger burrows have multiple entrances. Most trap-door spiders cover each entrance to the burrow with a door that opens and closes on a hinge of silk. The door may be as simple as a sheet of silk or as sturdy as a thick plug of earth, held together by silk and covered with leaves. A trap-door spider hunts by lying in wait just inside the entrance of its burrow. When it senses the vibrations of potential prey, it pounces and drags the passerby into the burrow.

Native to the Mediterranean islands of Corsica and Sardinia, *Cteniza sauvagesi* is a trapdoor spider that spends its life inside a silk-lined burrow, reaching out with its front legs to snatch passing prey

ARANEOMORPHS: ALMOST ALL SPIDERS

The great majority of spider species—about 90 percent of them—belong to the araneomorph suborder. Because the araneomorphs evolved more recently than the mesothelids and mygalomorphs, they are sometimes called the modern spiders or true spiders.

Araneomorph spiders' most distinctive feature is their chelicerae, or fangs. Instead of striking straight down like the fangs of spiders in the other two suborders, the fangs of modern spiders point inward and pivot toward each other, like a set of gripping pincers. In some species the fangs meet and cross. This lets the spiders pin and hold even tiny prey with great precision.

The world's largest and most recognizable spiders, the tarantulas, are in the mygalomorph group, but the world's smallest spiders are araneomorphs. Most of the dwarf spiders of the family Linyphiidae, for example, are smaller than 0.25 inch (0.6 centimeter) in length. The smallest spider of all may be *Patu marplesi*, a member of the family Symphytoganthidae, the dwarf orb-weavers. *P. marplesi* lives on certain Pacific islands. Males of the species have a legspan of just 0.018 inches (.46 millimeters), making them about the size of a period on this page.

Although most people will never see *P. marplesi*, nearly everyone occasionally encounters spiders in the course of everyday life. These spiders are likely to belong to the araneomorph subgroup. With around 95 families, the araneomorphs include a vast variety of spiders. There are

A small jumping spider has captured a fly. Soon the spider will suck out the softened insides of the unlucky insect.

large, roving types such as the long-legged wolf, huntsman, and wandering spiders, some of which can reach 2 inches (5 centimeters) in length. These hunting spiders, generally colored a drab gray or brown, are found in forests or fields.

Similar to wolf spiders and wandering spiders are the long-legged spiders of the Pisauridae family, sometimes called nursery-web spiders because they build tent-shaped webs for their young. Certain species of these forest-dwelling spiders, such as members of the genus *Dolomedes*, are also known as raft spiders or fishing spiders because they can walk on water. Their feet are equipped with long hairs that spread the spiders'

Dolomedes fimbriatus, a raft spider, spends much of its time on leaves near pools or brooks. It can walk on water to hunt minnows, water insects, and small salamanders.

weight over a large area. This lets the spiders prowl the water's surface, hunting for insects, minnows, and tadpoles.

Human buildings are a comfortable habitat for some types of araneomorph spiders. The tiny members of the family Oonopidae often live in houses, where they feed on even tinier insects—or on the remains of prey left behind by larger spiders. Daddy-long-legs spiders, which belong to the family Pholcidae, are also often found in houses, sheds, barns, and other structures. One common species, *Pholcus phalangoides*, builds fine, sparse webs called cobwebs in the corners of rooms.

Some araneomorph spiders, such as the small jumping spiders of the family Salticidae, have hard-looking carapaces on their cephalothoraxes. Others are smooth-bodied all over, or hairy. The kite spiders and thorn spiders, which belong to the family Araneidae, or orb weavers, have spines, spikes, or hornlike projections on their abdomens. These spines may make the spiders uninviting to potential predators, or they may

Trailing a strand of silk, a jumping spider leaps onto a fly.

disguise the spiders, giving them the appearance of long-jawed beetles, thorns, or dead leaves.

Many orb weavers are brightly colored, but the most colorful spiders are probably the crab spiders of the family Thomisidae. This is one of the largest spider families, with about 2,000 species worldwide. Around 250 species of crab spiders are found in the United States. Crab spiders do not build webs to catch prey. A few species move around, looking for something to eat, but most crab spiders are what scientists call ambush predators. They sit without moving, waiting for something edible to come to them.

Crab spiders occupy a wide range of environments, from deserts to tropical rain forests. They sometimes live in human dwellings, but their most common site for lying in ambush is a plant or flower. When a bee, ant, fly, or other insect visits the flower, the crab spider snatches the prey with its pedipalps and its first two pairs of legs, which have long, sharp hairs on their inner edges to improve the spider's grip.

Many crab spider species have protective coloration, which means that their coloring matches their usual backgrounds, helping them hide in plain sight. Species that usually live on tree bark have brown, rough-looking backs. Those that live

A crab spider on a Costa Rican plant mimicks a dried leaf. The spider's abdomen points upward. Its head is pointed downward, along the stem, and its legs are folded on each side.

A crab spider in Borneo is disguised as a bird dropping on a leaf. Its disguise may attract prey as well as discouraging possible predators.

among grass or leaves are green or brown, while desert species are speckled tan. A number of species are bright yellow, pink, or white to match the flowers they lurk among. A few are orange or reddish.

Misumena vatia is a species of crab spider that is common in Europe, Asia, and North America. In many parts of the world people know it as the common flower spider, but some Americans call it the goldenrod spider because its bright yellow coloring matches the weed known as goldenrod, in which this spider often sits. Yet *M. vatia* has the ability—very rare among spiders—to change color from yellow to white, if it moves to a white flower. If the spider later moves back to a yellow flower, it can change back to yellow, although the change takes a day or so.

A few crab spiders are called bird-dropping spiders. With lumpy, crusty-looking bodies colored black and white, they look like blobs of dried bird droppings. This disguise not only helps the spiders avoid birds and other predators, but it may even attract some kinds of prey, such as manure-loving flies.

SILK AND WEBS

Spiders are not the only animals that make silk. Some mites—also members of the arachnid order—can spin silk from their pedipalps. A number of insects produce silk when they are in their larval form, an early stage of their lives. They spin silk thread into cocoons in which they metamorphose, or change, into their adult forms. The silk industry, many centuries old, is based on the silk threads made by an insect larva called the silkworm.

To many people, however, silk calls up images of spiders, not of insect larvae. Spiders are the supreme weavers of the natural world. A dusty web stretching across a corner, or a web glistening with dewdrops as it hangs between two shrubs, is a universal symbol for a spider. Yet although all spiders can make silk, not all of them weave webs.

Spiders make silk by extruding, or pressing out, a liquid protein from glands inside their bodies. This substance leaves the spider's body through the abdominal glands called spinnerets, which are like movable turrets covered with tiny openings that extrude silk. When the liquid silk is pressed through the spinnerets and out into the air, it forms a thread that is both durable and strong. Some varieties of spider silk are believed to be as strong as steel wire of the same thickness—about one-fiftieth as thick as an average human hair, or less. As spiders spin the silk from their spinnerets, they comb it and arrange it with their rear pairs of legs.

Arachnologists have identified at least half a dozen types of spider silk. Some species of spiders make just one or two types, while others can make most types. Some spiders have a flat silk-producing organ called a cribellum in addition to their turretlike spinnerets. The cribellum may extrude silk from as many as 40,000 minute openings. Silk from this organ, called cribellate silk, is very thin. The spider may weave many strands of it into a fuzzy or woolly-looking thread that entangles the legs of prey. Other kinds of spiders lack the cribellum but can produce silk with sticky points along its length.

The orb weavers and a number of other kinds of spiders use their silk to build netlike traps for prey. Orb weavers create their webs in geo-metric patterns. The classic orb web consists of straight lines shooting out in all direc-tions from the center, with a long spiral line winding across them, although there are many variations. Other kinds of spiders make webs that look like sheets, tents, domes, or irregular tangles or mazes of silk. Webs of the sheet-web weavers in the family Agelenidae, a group of about 800 common house and garden spiders, can be so fine that they are almost invisible unless they happen

A young argiope spider has built a web with a stabilimentum, an area of thick, bright white silk. This part of the web is not sticky and does not capture prey. Some arachnologists think it may serve as a warning to keep birds from flying through the web and destroying the spider's work.

A large web can form when many spiders create individual webs close together. Sometimes the builders of these huge web masses belong to several different species. A spider that strays out of its own web may become its neighbor's prey.

to get wet. When a field or garden appears blanketed with webs on a damp morning, the agelenids have been at work.

If a spider's web is not destroyed, it can last as long as a year or so. Some webs become quite large if the spider keeps adding on to them. Occasionally many spiders build webs next to one another, giving the impression of a single huge, shared web. In the summer of 2007, for example, visitors to Texas's Lake Tawakoni State Park were astonished to see such a web stretching from tree to tree for 200 yards (180 meters). One of the largest webs ever recorded, it appeared in news stories around the world.

Webs are not the only way spiders catch prey with their silk. The net-casting spiders of the family Deinopidae weave small webs, which they hold between their front legs as they hang head-downwards from a few threads linking twigs or stems. They wait for insects to pass by

Spiders of the Sea

Sea spiders crawl across the ocean floor on eight (or more) legs, but they are not really spiders. They are not even arachnids. The thousand or so species of animals known as sea spiders belong to their own arthropod order, the pycnogonids. These small-bodied, long-legged creatures are found in all of the world's oceans, including the deep, cold Arctic and Antarctic waters. Most pycnogonids have four pairs of legs, but a few species have five or even six pairs. The largest species measure more than 20 inches (50 cm) from leg tip to leg tip, but most are much smaller. Like nearly all of the arachnids, the pycnogonids are carnivores. They roam about feeding on soft undersea creatures such as sponges and sea anemones. Even though sea spiders are not arachnids, it is easy to see how they got their name. In both appearance and behavior, they resemble the hunting spiders of the terrestrial world.

A brilliantly colored pycnogonid crawls across an ocean reef. Although they are often called sea spiders, pycnogonids are not spiders. They are not even arachnids, although they do belong to the arthropod phylum.

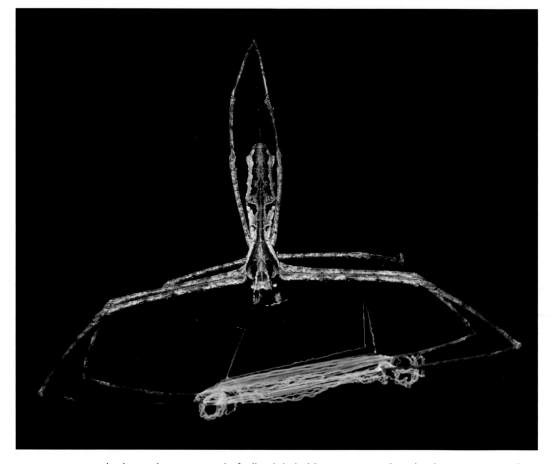

A net-casting spider hangs by one strand of silk while holding its net ready to be thrown over anything edible that ventures nearby.

beneath them and then scoop up the prey with the nets. Other spiders make fishing lines—lengths of silk with sticky ends. They swing these lines through the air to nab moths or other flying prey.

In addition to using silk to catch prey, spiders may use it to wrap up their prey to be eaten later; to make egg sacs (protective cases for their eggs); to create cocoons in which to hide while they molt, and to build nests for themselves and sometimes for their young. Small spiders use silk

In this series of photos, an argiope spider fashions an egg case out of silk. The silk will protect the spider's eggs from moisture and small predators. In some species, females tend their eggs cases until the young hatch.

to travel, flying through the air on strands like tiny parachutes, carried by the wind. Spiders' ability to spin and use silk in so many ways makes them unique in the animal world.

Tiny arachnids called red spider mites crawl over a larger arachnid, from a different order, called a harvestman. The mites are on dangerous territory—harvestmen often prey on mites.

From Scorpions to Dust Mites

Spiders are the most familiar arachnids to most people, but they are just one of the eleven orders of arachnids. The other ten orders contain thousands of arachnids that are the closest relatives of the spiders. These arachnids range in size from scorpions more than 8 inches (20 cm) long to dust mites so small that they cannot be seen without a magnifying glass or microscope.

SCORPIONS

The order Scorpiones contains between 1,500 and 2,000 species of scorpions. Most varieties are found in warm and hot regions of the world, but one species, *Paruroctonus boreus,* the northern scorpion, is found as far north as southern Canada.

Many scorpions are desert dwellers, but there are also species that inhabit forests, mountainous areas, caves, meadows, and suburban backyards. Scorpions are good burrowers, and nearly all species are nocturnal, or active at night. They typically spend the day in their burrows or lying quietly under logs, rocks, or tree bark. By night they either move around in search of prey or lie in wait to ambush prey that strays too close.

Scorpions are generally brown, yellow, or tan in color, although there are a few greenish or reddish species. They have long, flattened bodies covered with tough plates of chitin. Their pedipalps end in claws that work like pincers. The top prong of the claw is fixed and does not move, while the bottom prong moves up and down to pinch against the upper one. In some species the inner edges of the claws are serrated, or rough-edged like a saw blade.

The rear segments of a scorpion's abdomen form what is sometimes called the scorpion's tail. These segments are flexible, allowing the scorpion to arch its tail over its back. Scorpions deliver their venom by stinging,

With its abdomen arched upward, ready to sting, this South African scorpion is prepared to defend itself.

EXTERNAL ANATOMY OF A SCORPION

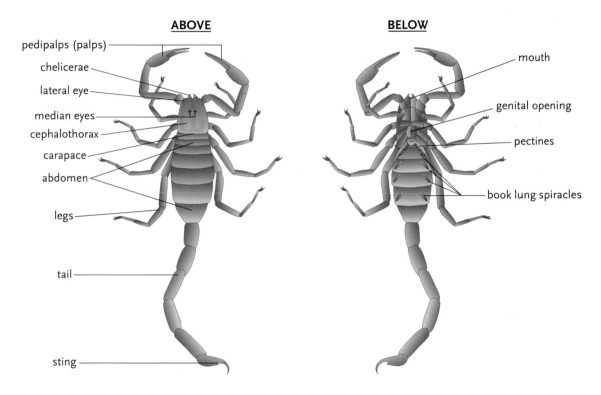

ABOVE

BELOW

pedipalps (palps)

chelicerae

lateral eye

median eyes

cephalothorax

carapace

abdomen

legs

tail

sting

mouth

genital opening

pectines

book lung spiracles

not biting. A scorpion's venom gland is located inside the last segment, which bears a sting. Some species use their venom only in self-defense and rely on their powerful pincers to crush and kill their prey. Other species grasp the prey with their pincers and then deliver a fatal sting.

A scorpion has a pair of eyes on the top of its head and one or more pairs of eyes along the sides. Scorpions do not have particularly good eyesight, however. Much more important to them is the ability to sense vibrations with the hairs on their bodies and legs. They also have a set of organs that no other arachnid possesses. Called pectines, these comblike organs are located on the underside of the scorpion's body, between the fourth pair of legs. They trail across the ground when the scorpion walks. Scientists think that they serve as additional vibration sensors. The

With a length of about 8 inches (20 cm), *Pandinus imperator* is one of the world's largest scorpions, but this emperor scorpion, as it is called, usually runs instead of fighting when threatened.

pectines may also play a role in scorpion reproduction by helping the animals detect the pheromones, or chemical signals, of potential mates.

Like other stinging, venomous animals, scorpions are a source of fear to many people. Scorpions, however, are rarely aggressive. They sting only when they are disturbed or feel threatened. People are most likely to be stung by a scorpion when they startle the animal, perhaps by placing a hand or foot near the scorpion without seeing it. Campers in dry, warm regions known to be scorpion habitat should carefully shake out shoes, sleeping bags, and other places where scorpions might have taken refuge.

Nearly all scorpion stings are painful, but very few are life-threatening. People at high risk of serious medical problems from scorpion stings include the very young, the frail elderly, and those with allergies to venom. Most of the scorpions whose stings are dangerous to human are found in the family Buthidae. Many reports of scorpion bites involve the fat-tailed scorpions, members of the genus *Androctonus*, because these species are common near human settlements and farms in North Africa and the Middle East. In contrast, the much larger African emperor scorpion, *Pandinus imperator,* is rarely known to sting people. When it does, its sting is not much more painful than that of a bee.

PSEUDOSCORPIONS

The order Pseudoscorpiones contains about 3,300 species. The name means "false scorpions" and comes from the fact that these arachnids look like small,

Two pseudoscorpions wave their venomous claws. These arachnids are not rare, but they are so small that people seldom notice them.

tailless scorpions. Compared with most scorpions, the pseudoscorpions are tiny. The largest species are just under 0.25 inch (0.6 cm) long.

These little arachnids are found on every continent except Antarctica. Although they tolerate cold weather better than true scorpions, they are most common in tropical or subtropical regions. Their typical habitats include tree bark, the leaf litter on the forest floor, the soil under rocks and logs, and caves. A few species live near the sea, in what scientists call the splash zone—the rocky or sandy area at the edge of waves. Several species, including *Chelifer cancroides,* are often found in houses and cellars, living in dark, undisturbed places. Like spiders, pseudoscorpions can make cocoons of silk or small nests of silk, but they do not have spinnerets. They spin the silk from glands in their jaws.

Pseudoscorpions have segmented abdomens, but their abdomens are round or blunt, not tapering to a "tail" as in true scorpions. Because pseudoscorpions have no tails, they cannot carry venom glands and stings in their tails like true scorpions. Instead, the pseudoscorpions have venom glands in their pedipalps, which have evolved into claws that both pinch and deliver venom. The pseudoscorpions' prey—insects and other small arachnids—includes ants, fruit flies, mites, lice, and moth larvae.

WHIP SCORPIONS

The order Uropygi contains about 100 arachnids known as whip scorpions, uropygids, or vinegaroons. That last name comes from the fact that many species in this order can spray an acid similar to vinegar (or, in some cases, a chemical that is more like chlorine) from glands at the back of their abdomens. They use this unpleasant spray to defend themselves from predators such as birds, snakes, and lizards.

Whip scorpions have flat, brownish bodies with long, whiplike tails. The largest arachnids in this order measure about 2.75 inches (7

The uropygid's most distinctive features are its long, slender tail and its long first pair of legs, which it uses like antennae to feel its way. Uropygids are known as whip scorpions and vinegaroons. Some people in the American South call this arachnid a grampus.

cm) in length, not counting the tail, which may be nearly as long as the body. The whip scorpions have short, sturdy, clawed pedipalps for crushing prey and digging tunnels. They use their long, thin first pair of legs like antennae to feel the ground ahead as they move. Found in leaf litter, rotting logs, and soil in India, Southeast Asia, and the tropical and subtropical Americas, whip scorpions are nocturnal hunters that eat worms, slugs, cockroaches, crickets, and other small ground-dwelling creatures.

MICROWHIP SCORPIONS

The 80 or so known species of microwhip scorpions are classified in the order Palpigradi. These little-known arachnids are extremely small. The largest measure barely 0.1 inch (3 millimeters) in length.

Microwhip scorpions are flat, light-colored, and segmented, with small whiplike tails. They live in damp, moist soil, usually under rocks and logs, and they prey on tiny soil-dwelling arthropods. All species so far discovered are eyeless. Arachnologists think that there are probably many more species of microwhip scorpions waiting to be identified.

SHORT-TAILED OR SPLIT-MIDDLE WHIP SCORPIONS

The order Schizomida contains more than 230 species of arachnids, called the short-tailed or split-middle whip scorpions. Some species are slightly larger than the microwhip scorpions, reaching lengths of almost 0.2 inches (5 mm).

Arachnids in the order Schizomida have short whiplike tails. The carapace on top of their cephalothoraxes is split down the middle, or divided into two plates. The first pair of walking legs has evolved into a set of antennalike sense organs. Like the microwhip scorpions, the short-tailed whip scorpions are eyeless. They are similar to the microwhips in other ways, too. They live in the upper layers of soil and in dark, damp places under rocks and logs.

HOODED TICK SPIDERS

The order Ricinulei contains about sixty species of arachnids that are usually called hooded tick spiders, although they are neither ticks nor spiders. These eyeless predators are similar in habitat and behavior to split-tailed whip scorpions and microwhip scorpions. They live in damp, dark conditions and are usually found in soil, where they feed on small insects and other arthropods.

Measuring 0.2 to 0.4 inches (5 to 10 mm) in length, hood tick spiders or ricinuleids have a movable segment of carapace at the front of the body that can be raised and lowered. When fully lowered, this "hood" covers the

The tiny, eyeless arachnids known as hooded tick spiders are neither ticks nor spiders. They are called "hooded" because they can cover their mouthparts with part of their carapace.

arachnid's chelicerae and mouth. Ricinuleids have narrow waists and large abdomens for their size. Their pedipalps form pincers. When ricinuleids mate, the males use their third pair of legs to transfer packets of sperm to the bodies of the females.

WHIP SPIDERS

The order Amblypygi contains about 135 species of arachnids that are known as whip spiders, amblypygids, cave spiders, or tailless whip scorpions. Amblypygids are native to tropical and subtropical regions around the world.

Amblypygids, also called whip spiders or tailless whip scorpions, use their long front legs to feel for prey as they walk around, often moving sideways. This whip spider has just molted. Its discarded skin rests above it.

Like the uropygids, whip scorpions use their first pair of legs as long, antennalike sense organs. In amblypygids these legs are often considerably longer than the body. They are also highly movable. The amblypygid can aim each of its first legs in a different direction at the same time, in order to feel ahead, to the side, and even behind itself. These arachnids are also well equipped with eyes—they have two eyes in the middle of the head and three on each side.

Whip spiders have flattened, segmented bodies with carapaces, brown or tan in color. They lack tails, but they have spiny pedipalps for clutching their prey, which consists of insects and arthropods. Their length ranges from less than 0.25 inch to about 2.5 inches (0.6 to 6 cm).

SUN SPIDERS

The 1,000 or so species in the order Solifugae are sometimes called solifugids. Sun spider and wind scorpion are their most common names, although these arachnids are neither spiders nor scorpions. U.S. soldiers in the Middle East, where solifugids are common, often call them camel spiders.

The name *Solifugae* means "those that run away from the Sun," and solifugids often seek shade, although some species are diurnal, or active by day. These arachnids live in warm parts of Asia, Africa, southern Europe, and the Americas. Their favored habitats are deserts or dry grasslands and woodlands. They dig burrows or pits to escape the heat, and females lay their eggs in these retreats.

The biggest species of solifugids have body lengths of 2.5 inches (6.4 cm) and legspans of about 5 inches (12.7 cm), although many species are considerably smaller. All species have large chelicerae that operate like pincers. Their pedipalps are long and sturdy. The sun spiders use the palps like an extra pair of legs, which can make them appear to have ten legs. The legs and bodies of most solifugids are hairy, with bristles that are sensitive to vibrations. The bristles also help support the animals in soft or loose sand.

Solifugids, sometimes called solifuges, solpugids, or camel spiders, are common in the Middle East. These fast-moving, lively hunters lack venom but are armed with powerful chelicerae.

Solifugids are active hunters. They are the fastest-moving arachnids, often seen zigzagging across the sand or running up a tree. Their pedipalps and feet have small structures like suction cups. These give the solifugids an excellent grip on struggling prey as well as on sheer climbing surfaces such as walls.

Because some species of solifugids are large and active, they can be highly visible. During U.S. military actions in the Middle East, these arachnids have become the subject of many myths among soldiers who are not familiar with them. The camel spiders, as troops call them, are said to be able to outrun jeeps, to scream, to attack camels, and to feed on the flesh of sleeping people. None of these tales is true. Solifugids do not even have venom glands. Their bites can be painful because of their large fangs and because of the possibility of infection, but sun spiders do not attack anything larger than a small lizard or bird.

HARVESTMEN

Abut 6,400 species of arachnids belong to the order Opiliones, or harvestmen. Scientists know from comparing modern harvestmen with 400-year-old fossils that this order of arachnids has not changed much over a long stretch of time.

Harvesten are sometimes known as daddy-long-legs. Although harvestmen are not the same as the pholcid family of spiders, which are also called daddy-long-legs spiders, both groups of arachnids have similar shapes: small bodies and very long, thin legs.

Phalangium opilio, a common species of harvestman, is useful to farmers because it eats destructive pests, including aphids, leafhoppers, mites, and beetle larvae.

Depending on the species, harvestmen's bodies may be narrow, oval, round and buttonlike, or even wedge-shaped or triangular. The largest bodies measure just under 0.5 inch (about 1.2 cm) in length, and many are smaller than that. Legs, however, can reach lengths of 6 inches (15.2 cm), although some species have short legs. The legs have seven segments and are quite flexible. Some species have spines on their legs for defense. The second pair of legs may be longer than the rest—many species of harvestmen use these legs as sensory antennae. The legs are easily detached, and harvestmen are sometimes seen with fewer than six legs. They can lose one or even two legs to birds or other predators and still be able to move around.

Most species of harvestmen have small chelicerae and short pedipalps. They generally have two eyes, which are sometimes mounted on tiny turrets or stalks at the front of their heads. Scientists think that harvestmen do not see images; instead, their eyes simply see light. A few species, including some that live in caves, have no eyes. Many harvestmen have a form of chemical self-defense: glands in the cephalothorax that squirt smelly liquids if the arachnids are threatened.

Members of the opilionid order do not have venom glands, and they do not produce silk. Their feeding habits set them apart from spiders and other arachnids. Nearly all arachnids are predators that feed on live animals, but harvestmen's diets are more varied. Some species are hunters, either prowling in search of prey or lying ready to ambush a passing small insect. Many harvestmen, however, eat plant matter or fungi. Often they scavenge on decaying plants or animals, or on animal feces. Unlike all other arachnids, harvestmen do not have to digest their food outside their bodies. They can take in small pieces of solid food.

MITES AND TICKS

The order Acari (sometimes called Acarina) contains at least 30,000 known species of mites and ticks. Some arachnologists estimate the number of

Deadly Daddy-Long-Legs?

Have you heard about the daddy-long-legs? Its venom, people say, is the deadliest in the world. The only thing that keeps people from being killed by daddy-long-legs is the fact that the fangs of the daddy-long-legs are too small and weak to break human flesh!

If you *have* heard about the deadly venom and feeble fangs of the daddy-long-legs, you've heard an urban myth. This piece of misinformation about daddy-long-legs has been spreading for years, but there is no truth to it.

"Daddy-long-legs" can refer to two different groups of arachnids. The first is the order of opilionids, or harvestmen. Harvestmen, which are sometimes called daddy-long-legs, are almost always found outdoors. They eat both vegetable and animal matter, but they do not have deadly venom. They don't even have venom glands.

The second kind of daddy-long-legs is the pholcid family of spiders, known as cellar spiders or daddy-long-legs spiders. Like harvestmen, pholcids have long, slender legs and small bodies, but they are often seen indoors. When most people think of "daddy-long-legs," they are thinking of these spiders. Pholcids have short fangs. Experts do not know whether or not they can bite people, but there is no medical or scientific record of pholcid bites harming any mammal, from a mouse to a person. As far as scientists know, pholcid spiders have fangs and venom that can kill their small insect prey, but nothing more.

A female cellar spider shares her web with her spiderlings. This and other spiders in the pholcid family are sometimes called daddy-long-legs, as are harvestmen.

species at 45,000 to 50,000. The difference comes about partly because of disagreements about species classification. Species that have been identified on the basis of just a few specimens occasionally turn out to be duplicates of other species. In addition, some estimates include specimens that have been collected but not yet fully studied. All experts, however, agree that the number of *unknown* species of mites and ticks is probably much higher still.

As scientists learn more about mites and ticks, they are beginning to change the taxonomic classification of these arachnids. Traditionally mites and ticks have been combined in the order Acari, but some arachnologists now consider Acari to be a subclass of arachnids. Within the Acari they divide the mites and ticks into two or even three orders.

Most mites are very small, measuring 0.03 inch (0.76 mm) or less in length. Some, such as the house dust mites of the genus *Dermatophagoides,* are microscopic, invisible to the unaided eye. The smallest mites are the gall-forming mites, which are about eight-thousandths of an inch (less than .2 mm) long. Some scientists think that these mites are not just the smallest arachnids in the world but the smallest arthropods.

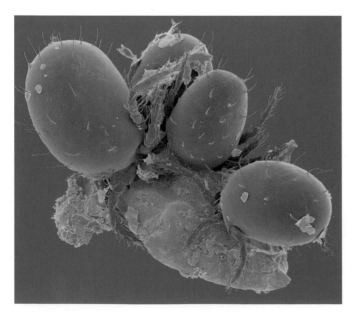

Certain mites, however, are considerably larger and can be easily seen. Chigger mites reach lengths of about 0.125

The larvae of chigger mites, magnified 26 times by an electron microscope, devour a piece of human skin.

inch (3 mm). The largest mites belong to the family Trombidiidae. Usually red or orange, these arachnids are called velvet mites for their thick coats of short, plushy hair. Velvet mites can be almost 0.5 inch (1.27 cm) long.

Mites generally have roundish, unsegmented bodies. Their legs may be short or curled under the body. Adults usually have four pairs of legs, like other arachnids, but a few species have fewer legs.

Of all the arachnids, mites have colonized the greatest diversity of habitats. They are found everywhere that other arachnids live, and they are also found in places where no other arachnids live. Mites live on glaciers and polar icecaps, as well as deep in the soil in all parts of the world. They are also aquatic. Free-swimming mites live in both fresh and salt water. Mites have even been found in the steaming, chemical-rich waters of hot springs.

Red spider mites, which can spin webs of very fine silk, infest a leaf. These mites are a significant pest on agricultural and ornamental plants.

Mites' feeding habits are as diverse as their habitats. Some of them, such as the spider mites of the family Tetranychidae, eat the leaves and stems of living plants. Spider mites are among the few mites that can make silk. They sometimes cover the plants they have infested with sheets of web.

Beetle mites of the family Cryptostigmata eat dead plant matter. These and many other kinds of mites are called detritivores, which means that they eat detritus, dead or cast-off material. By aiding in the decomposition of dead plants and animals, detritivore mites play an important role in recycling organic material in the world's ecosystem and maintaining healthy soils. House dust mites are detritivores, too. Their genus name *Dermatophagiodes* means "eaters of skin," and their main food is the tiny flakes of skin that humans shed all the time.

Some mites are predators, feeding on other small arthropods such as insects. Others eat mold, which is a type of fungus. Many mites are parasites, which means that they live on, or inside, larger animals. The parasites feed on the blood or flesh of their host organisms. Several kinds of mites, for example, parasitize honeybees. Many other insects are hosts to parasitic mites as well. Some mites are small enough to live inside the ear cavities of moths.

Dust mites, magnified by 25 times, hunt for human skin scales in a piece of woolen cloth. These mites number in the millions in most residences. They are invisible, but their presence can trigger allergic reactions in some people.

Reptiles, birds, and mammals—including humans—are also parasitized by mites. Scabies mites of the family Sarcoptidae, for example, live on people and other mammals. They live among hairs, or even inside hollow hair shafts, and feed by chewing small tunnels in the host's skin. Infestations of these mites cause the diseases known as scabies and mange. Mites in the family Dermanyssidae live as parasites on both birds and mammals, using their sharp, tiny chelicerae to puncture the skin so that the mites can consume blood.

Not all the mites found on insects, birds, and other animals are parasites. Some are simply hitchhikers, practicing a way of moving around that scientists call phoresy. These mites use their legs or mouthparts to fasten themselves onto larger animals in order to travel from place to place. When they reach a suitable new habitat, they release their grip. Mites that feed on flower pollen, for example, travel from flower to flower by crawling onto the hummingbirds that visit the flowers to drink nectar.

Ticks are parasites. All tick species are hematophages, or blood drinkers, that prey on reptiles, birds, or mammals. Some parasitize just one or two species of host animals. Other ticks attach themselves to any host they can find.

Because ticks stick their mouthparts into their hosts' bloodstreams, they can pass blood cells from one host to another. When they do this, ticks can spread disease organisms carried in the blood—such as bacteria, viruses, and other small parasitic organisms—from one host to another. Ticks transmit many diseases that affect humans, including Lyme disease, tularemia, Rocky Mountain spotted fever, and meningoencephalitis. They also infect livestock and pets with disease.

Although some ticks are extremely small, most are larger than mites. One of the largest species is the Lone Star tick, *Amblyomma americanum,* which lives in the central United States. It may reach lengths of almost 0.5 inch (1.27 cm). All tick species are larger after feeding because their bodies swell up as they fill with blood from the host. After a full meal a tick may be two or three times its normal size.

A female Lone Star tick perches atop a plant stalk, waiting to hitch a ride on a warm-blooded host, which will also provide the tick's meals.

There are two main types of ticks, hard and soft. Hard ticks belong to the family Ixodidae. Their flattened bodies are coated with thick layers of chitin that is tough, leathery, and hard to crush. Hard ticks may remain on hosts, fixed in place by gluey saliva, for days at a time. Some hard ticks, such as the brown dog tick, *Rhipicephalus sanguineus,* remain on the same host throughout its life.

Soft ticks belong to the family Argasidae. They are covered by thin membranes of chitin and are usually round. These ticks attach themselves to hosts for brief feedings, then drop off. Often they live in a host bird or animal's nest or burrow, so that they can feed repeatedly from the same host. These ticks are also able to go for long stretches without eating—up to a year or more between meals in some species.

Ticks do not jump or fly. They find hosts by waiting on grasses, shrubs, or trees for a suitable host to brush against them or pass underneath so that they can climb or drop aboard.

A typical tick life cycle begins when an adult female tick draws her last meal of blood, falls off her host, lays a large mass of eggs—as many as 4,000 in some species—in the soil, and then dies. The eggs hatch into tiny larvae that do not yet have all four pairs of legs. These larvae, sometimes called seed ticks, wait on grass stems or leaves. The larvae that find a host take their first meal, then molt into nymphs: miniature eight-legged versions of their adult forms. After another feeding, the nymphs molt into adults. These stages may take place on different hosts or on the same host. Depending upon the species, the tick's lifespan is from one to three years. Its life cycle is just one of many patterns found in the arachnid class.

Dermacentor variabilis, the wood tick or American dog tick, clings to strands of animal hair. This species of tick transmits several diseases, including Rocky Mountain spotted fever, to humans.

73

A female wolf spider carries her newly hatched young, known as nymphs or spider-lings, on her body. Once they have molted, the young spiders are ready for life on their own. They will leave their mother, who might eat them if she saw them again.

The Lives of Arachnids

Most spiders live just one year—sometimes less. Large mygalomorph spiders such as tarantulas, however, have been known to live for more than ten years in the wild and for twenty-five or more years in captivity. These spiders do not reach full maturity until they are six or seven years old.

Some scorpions have been reported to live twenty or twenty-five years as well, although the lifespans of most species are about four years. Scientists do not yet know, however, how long most of the smaller arachnids usually live. The lifespans of these animals are just one of many mysteries that remain to be solved by arachnologists.

REPRODUCTION

One aspect of arachnid life that scientists have studied in some detail is reproduction. Arachnids have evolved a broad diversity of methods for mating and giving birth to their young.

Harvestmen are the only arachnid order in which the males have penises, sex organs that enter the bodies of females to deposit sperm. In all

This web contains a female black widow spider, her egg sac, and the much smaller male of the species.

other arachnid orders, males and females have genital openings on the undersides of their abdomens. The males deposit their sperm on the ground or on their bodies, either in liquid form or in little packets called spermatophores. Mating occurs when the female picks up the sperm and inserts it into her genital opening, or when the male uses his chelicerae, pedipalps, or legs to insert it into her. Male spiders, for example, pass liquid sperm into females with their palps. Male sun spiders or solifugids use their fangs to put droplets of sperm into females' bodies.

Male spiders of some species use signals to tell females that they are interested in mating. They may pluck a strand of the female's web in a certain way, or raise their palps or legs in the air. Some male tarantulas make a whistling sound. These and other male spiders often approach their potential mates with caution—and rightly so. Females are usually larger than males and may be aggressive. Scientists have seen male spiders eaten

A male velvet mite follows the larger female. In some species of mites, males fight over small, immature females and then wait for the females to mature.

as prey before they had a chance to mate. Others get eaten afterward. Usually, however, male spiders simply leave after mating. In a few species, such as sheet-web weavers of the genus *Tenegaria,* males live together with females in the females' webs for some time after mating.

Male mites sometimes fight tiny but fierce battles over nymphs, or immature females. The winner guards the female and mates with her as soon as she molts into her adult form. Crab spiders do the same thing. The victorious male may refresh himself with a snack while waiting for the female to molt—he eats the rival he has defeated.

Ticks have several reproductive arrangements. Among hard ticks, males usually mate with females who are feeding on their hosts—the males, in fact, may feed on the females rather than on the hosts. Mating occurs when the male uses his mouthparts to place a large spermatophore in the female's body. For a female hard tick, this single mating is enough to fertilize as many as 10,000 eggs. Soft ticks have a different strategy. They mate many times. Each time, a few eggs are fertilized.

Scorpions species appear to fight, dance, or both when they are mating. Males and females of some species start by stinging each other repeatedly. Scientists think that this may arouse their reproductive urges. In other species the male and female scorpions simply swat each other with their tails instead of stinging. After the combat phase of the relationship, the male scorpion faces the female, grips her claws with his, and moves her around. This "dance of the scorpions" is sometimes called a courtship ritual, but by the time the scorpions have locked claws, the courtship phase is over. The male has already deposited a spermatophore on the ground. He is simply trying to shove or drag the female into position above it, so that she will pick it up.

Female ticks and their egg masses. Depending upon the species, a female tick may lay up to 10,000 eggs.

Not all scorpions engage in the reproductive dance. A few species reproduce without sex or mating. These species have no males. The females' eggs simply ripen into female young. In this type of reproduction, called parthenogenesis, females reproduce genetic copies of themselves. Parthenogenesis takes place in some insect species and other animals, but among the arachnids it is found only in the scorpion order.

Scorpions are unique among arachnids in another way as well. Whether they reproduce sexually or by parthenogenesis, scorpions are viviparous, meaning that they give birth to live young—anywhere from six miniature scorpions to more than 100 of them. All other arachnids are oviparous, which means that they lay eggs.

Some arachnids deposit their eggs and never see them again. Other mothers tend their eggs and are present when the young hatch. Depending on the type of arachnid, females may deposit their eggs individually around their territory; lay them in a pit, nest, or burrow; enclose them in a cocoon; or carry them around in an egg sac.

PARENTING AND SOCIAL LIFE

Parental care is part of life for many arachnids. In some species of mites, for example, males and females cooperate to guard their eggs and young from predators, including other mites. Wolf spiders—and some other spiders as well—carry their eggs sacs around with them. When the eggs hatch, the tiny spiderlings climb up their mother's legs and onto her back, where they cling to hairs. They ride around this way until they are ready for their first molt. At that time the young spiders scramble off, each one ready to begin life on its own.

Female amblypygids and uropygids, better known as whip spiders and whip scorpions, also carry their young around on their backs. So do scorpions. Solifugid or sun spider mothers protect the burrows that contain their fifty or so eggs and young. Again, though, when the young reach their first molt, the period of parental care ends.

A Brazilian funnel-web spider, *Ischnothele caudata,* has been seen caring for its newly hatched young in a way that has not been observed in any other mygalomorph spider. For five weeks after the spiderlings hatch, they remain in the mother's web, and she regularly brings prey to them, placing it in the web and plucking strands of silk to get their attention. Female scorpions are also known to offer prey to their newly hatched young.

Aside from mating and, in some species, caring for their young, arachnids lead fairly solitary lives. Hundreds, thousands, or even millions of members of the same species may live close to one another, but they do not form complex social structures like the communities of ants, bees, termites, and other social insects. Sometimes they prey on one another—most arachnids are cannibals that will eagerly eat their own kinds. At other

Baby scorpions ride around on their mother's body for a short time after birth. Scorpions are the only arachnids to give birth to live young rather than eggs.

Anelosimus eximius, a South American spider, is one of the few known species of truly social arachnids. Hundreds or even thousands of these spiders live in large colonies like this shared web. They work together to tend egg sacs, repair the web, and catch prey, but they do not prey on each other.

times they simply ignore or tolerate each other, relying on chemical cues and vibrations to mark their territory and keep their distance from one another.

PEOPLE AND ARACHNIDS

Throughout the ages humans have had a love-hate relationship with arachnids. On one hand, people have feared spiders and scorpions for their bites and stings, even though the great majority of arachnids are harmless to humans. Some people find arachnids not just frightening but disgusting or creepy. In some cases, people can overcome these feelings of arachnophobia by learning more about arachnids or spending time around them.

The rare deaths caused by spiders or scorpions are not the biggest danger that arachnids pose to human life. Arachnids do far more damage by spreading disease and destroying crops. Mites and ticks carry a wide variety of diseases that can affect people. These arachnid-related health problems range from allergies caused by house dust mites to life-threatening diseases such as typhus (spread by some Asian chigger mites), Lyme disease, and other tick-borne illnesses.

Mites can cause serious economic damage when they infest orchards or farm fields and begin feeding on the liquids in plant leaves and stems.

A large wolf spider crawling through fall leaves may inspire fear, but it is mites and ticks, not spiders, that do real damage to humans.

An infestation by pests such as spider mites can quickly kill even large trees. Even when mites do not completely destroy crops, they can reduce their value. The citrus rust mite, for example, feeds or orange peels, and the oranges that are affected by the mites develop a brownish tint that makes them less desirable to buyers. Mites and ticks can also harm livestock and other economically useful animals. Varroa mites are parasites on honeybees and may spread crippling diseases among these insects.

Yet for all the problems they cause, arachnids have also been admired—especially spiders, for their skill as weavers. Myths and legends of many cultures feature spiders as wise or clever figures, such as the trickster Anansi in traditional African tales or the Spider Woman of Native American stories. In some of these stories the spider teaches humans the art of weaving cloth, or weaves a ladder that links the earth to the heavens. Folk tales from many countries cast spiders in the role of protectors. By quickly weaving a web across the entrance to a cave in which a hero is hiding from his enemies, the humble spider convinces the enemies that the cave must be empty. The hero could not have entered the cave, they think, without breaking the web.

People have used arachnids, especially spiders and scorpions, in a variety of ways. Doctors in Europe used to treat illnesses with potions or powders made from spiders that were thought to have healing properties. Traditional folk medicines in some parts of the world still use spiders and scorpions. Although most of these folk remedies have no real medicinal value, some contain venom-based ingredients that are medically active. In

In the heart of Beijing, Chinese fast-food choices include scorpion-on-a-stick.

Crab spiders are both beautiful and beneficial—they eat aphids and other insects that damage plants.

recent years, researchers studying arachnid venom have discovered chemical compounds that are now used in medicines for pain relief and to treat conditions such as heart disease.

To most Americans, the idea of eating a spider sounds like a bad episode of a reality show. In parts of Asia and South America, however, people eat large spiders, usually members of the tarantula family, as sources of protein. Roasted spider, say some who have tried it, tastes a little like chicken.

Tarantulas, along with some other species of spiders and scorpions, are also in growing demand as pets. Certain species of tarantulas can easily be handled, and some people think that they make good pets. Commerce in Mexican red-kneed tarantulas and a handful of other species started growing in the 1980s. By the 1990s some countries started regulating the spider trade, fearing that too many spiders were being harvested from the wild. Today communities in Mexico and elsewhere are experimenting with spider and scorpion ranching, raising the most desirable species in captivity to supply the pet trade.

More uses for arachnids may lie ahead. Agricultural researchers are investigating the possible use of arachnids for pest control. Although mites are pests on some crops, other arachnids, such as harvestmen, devour large numbers of mites and other pests as well. Organic farmers, and others who want to control pests without adding costly and potentially harmful chemicals to the environment, are looking for ways of encouraging helpful arachnids to populate their fields.

Farmers are not the only ones to benefit from the activities of arachnids. All of us benefit from the presence of spiders in our homes and yards. Every day, arachnids around the world kill uncountable quantities of mosquitoes and flies. Even an arachnophobe might agree that spiders are worth having around for that reason alone.

The long history of arachnids proves that these adaptable arthropods can live in a wide variety of conditions. The chances are good that arachnids will remain in existence for a long time to come.

The Future of Arachnids

These days the news seems full of disturbing stories about endangered animals on the brink of extinction. What about arachnids? Are they at risk of becoming extinct?

The good news is that arachnids don't seem to be in immediate trouble. Each year the World Conservation Union (IUCN), an international group of organizations devoted to biology and conservation, publishes the Red List, which identifies the species of plants and animals around the world that are most at risk. The 2007 Red List had just one arachnid—*Adelocosa anops,* the Kauai cave spider of Hawaii—in the Endangered category. Seven spiders, one harvestman, and one pseudoscorpion were listed as Vulnerable, or at risk of becoming endangered. Overall, arachnids were in much better shape on the Red List than most other classes of animals.

The bad news, though, is that the scientists who put together the Red List had reliable population data for just a handful of arachnid species. Many species of arachnids are so little known that researchers cannot estimate the size and overall well-being of their populations. Even for some well-known arachnids, information about the size of populations is scarce, or it does not exist at all.

Species that are found in many parts of the world, or that occur in enormous numbers—such as a million or more mites in a square yard (square meter) of forest floor—are unlikely to become endangered. Some arachnologists, though, fear that other species may be in trouble. Arachnids whose range is limited to a single small area, or who are harvested in great numbers for the pet trade, could be at special risk. Experts who have performed detailed species surveys in settings such as alpine meadows or the treetops in tropical forests know that there are new arachnid species to be found in almost every location. Many of these yet-unknown arachnids may live in limited ranges and habitats—perhaps as limited as a single stand of trees.

Conservationists also point out that large-scale environmental changes, such as habitat loss and global warming, may threaten arachnid species along with many other kinds of life. If that happens, many kinds of arachnids could become extinct before scientists have even discovered them.

A Kauai cave spider, or cave wolf spider, carries her young on her back. These seldom-seen arachnids face an uncertain future as an endangered species.

abdomen—The rear section of an arachnid's body; also called the opisthosoma.

adapt—To change or develop in ways that aid survival in the environment.

anatomy—The physical structure of an organism.

appendage—A limb or outgrowth of the body, such as a leg.

aquatic—Having to do with water; living in water (fresh or salt).

arachnid—An arthropod with six pairs of appendages (including four pairs of legs) and a body that is divided into two parts.

arachnology—The study of arachnids.

arboreal—Living in trees.

arthropod—An animal that has jointed appendages and an exoskeleton, or tough outer casing, instead of an internal skeleton; includes insects, crustaceans, and arachnids.

cephalothorax—The front section of an arachnid body; also called the prosoma.

chelicerae—The first pair of an arachnid's appendages, used to grip or bite prey.

conservation—Action or movement aimed at protecting and preserving wildlife or its habitat.

diurnal—Active by day.

evolution—The pattern of change in life-forms over time, as new species, or types of plants and animals, develop from old ones.

evolve—To change over time.

extinct—No longer existing; died out.

exoskeleton—The outer covering of an arthropod's body, made of a material called chitin; it may be a hard shell, as in crabs, or a softer protective casing, as in spiders.

genetic—Having to do with genes, material made of DNA inside the cells of living organisms. Genes carry information about inherited characteristics from parents to offspring and determine the form of each organism.

invertebrate—An animal that does not have a backbone; includes arthropods, worms, snails.

nocturnal—Active by night.

organism—Any living thing.

paleontology—The study of ancient life, mainly through fossils.

parasite—Animal that feeds on, and often lives on or inside, another animal.

pedipalps—The second pair of an arachnid's appendages; may be used as legs, antennae, or pincers, depending on the species.

spinneret—Silk-producing organ on the abdomen of a spider.

taxonomy—The scientific system for classifying living things, grouping them in categories according to similarities and differences, and naming them.

terrestrial—Living on the land.

venom—Poison in an arachnid's bite, used for self-defense and for stunning, paralyzing, or killing prey.

ARACHNID

PHYLUM

SUBPHYLUM

CLASS

Schizomida
(short-tailed or
split-middle
whip scorpions)

230 species*

Amblypygi
(whip spiders
or tailless
whip scorpions)

135 species*

Palpigradi
(microwhip
scorpions)

80 species*

ORDER

Uropygi
(whip scorpions)

100 species*

Araneae
(spiders)

40,000 species*

FAMILY TREE

Arthropoda (arthropods)

Chelicerata (arthropods with chelicerae)

Arachnida (arachnids)

Acari
(mites and ticks)
30,000+ species*

Solifugae
(sunspiders,
camel spiders,
wind scorpions,
solpugids)
1,000 species*

Scorpiones
(scorpions)
2,000 species*

Ricinulei
(hooded
tick spiders)
60 species*

Opiliones
(harvestmen,
daddy-long-legs)
6,400 species*

Pseudoscorpiones
(pseudoscorpions)
3,300 species*

*The number of species in each order and the total number of known arachnid species are approximations. Scientists' estimates vary widely. In addition, many species have yet to be identified.

FURTHER READING

Colligan, L.H. *Tick-Borne Illnesses.* New York: Marshall Cavendish Benchmark, 2008.

Gilpin, Daniel. *Centipedes, Millipedes, Scorpions & Spiders.* Minneapolis: Compass Point Books, 2005.

Hillyard, Paul. *Spiders.* New York: Facts On File, 2004.

Solway, Andrew. *Deadly Spiders and Scorpions.* Chicago: Heinemann, 2005.

Townsend, John. *Incredible Arachnids.* Chicago: Raintree, 2005.

Zabludoff, Marc. *Spiders.* New York: Marshall Cavendish Benchmark, 2006.

WEB SITES

http://www.everythingabout.net/articles/biology/animals/arthropods/arachnids
The kid-friendly Everything About Arachnids page offers a brief overview of the arachnid class, with additional pages on most of the orders within the class.

http://www.washington.edu/burkemuseum/spidermyth/myths/arach-nid.html
The University of Washington's Burke Museum sponsors the Spider Myths page, which gives the facts behind many common myths and misunderstandings about arachnids.

http://www.amonline.net.au/spiders
The Australian Museum Online has an excellent site devoted to spiders; although the emphasis is on Australia's own species, the site covers everything from spider biology to spiders in culture.

http://www.americanarachnology.org/AAS_information.html
The website of the American Arachnological Society offers information about arachnids, including a gallery of photographs of species in all eleven orders.

http://animals.nationalgeographic.com/animals/a-to-z.html?nav=TOP-NAV
The National Geographic Online site's A-to-Z index is a gateway to short articles on a variety of arachnids, including deer ticks, tarantulas, scorpions, black widow spiders, and the Egyptian giant solpugid.

http://evolution.berkeley.edu/evolibrary/article/0_0_0/arthropodstory
This interactive, kid-friendly overview of how arthropods (including arachnids) evolved is part of the University of California at Berkeley's excellent Understanding Evolution site.

The author found these books and articles helpful when researching this book.

Barth, Frederick G. *A Spider's World: Senses and Behavior.* Trans. M.A. Biedermann-Thorson. Boston: Verlag, 2001.

BBC News Online. "Scariest spider 'really a crab.'" February 15, 2005, http://news.bbc.co.uk/2/hi/uk_news/england/manchester/4268363.stm

Eisner, Thomas, et al. *Secret Weapons: Defenses of Insects, Spiders, Scorpions, and Other Many-Legged Creatures.* Cambridge, MA: Harvard University Press, 2005.

Harvey, Mark S. "The Neglected Cousins: What Do We Know About the Smaller Arachnid Orders?" *Journal of Arachnology,* 2002, Volume 30, pp. 357-372.

Mason, Adrienne. *The World of the Spider.* San Francisco: Sierra Club Books, 1999.

McGavin, George C. *Smithsonian Handbooks: Insects, Spiders, and Other Terrestrial Arthropods.* New York: Dorling Kindersley, 2002.

Preston-Mafham, Rod and Ken Preston-Mafham. *Encyclopedia of Insects and Spiders.* San Diego, CA: Thunder Bay Press, 2005.

Morse, Douglas. *A Predator Upon a Flower: Life History and Fitness In a Crab Spider.* Cambridge, MA: Harvard University Press, 2007.

Rayor, Linda S. "Family Ties: Unexpected Social Behavior in an Improbable Arachnid, the Whip Spider." *Natural History,* February 2007, Vol. 116, Issue 1, pp. 38-44.

Walter, David Evans and Heather C. Proctor. *Mites: Ecology, Evolution, and Behavior.* New York: CABI, 1999.

I N D E X

Page numbers in **boldface** are illustrations.

Amblypygi, 62-63
aphids, 84-85
Arachne, 7-8
araneomorph, 40-46, **41,
      42, 43, 44, 45**
arthropods, 19-23

binomial nomenclature,
      10
book lungs, 27

camouflage, 44-45, **44, 45**
cephalothorax, 23, 25, 34
chelicerae, 25, 40
classification, 8-15, **16-17,
      90-91**
claws, 26, **26,** 54
cribellum, 46-47

daddy-long-legs, 43, 65-
      66, **65,** 67, **67**

egg, 50, 78, **78,** 79
      sac, 50, **76,** 79
endangerment, 86-87, **87**
evolution, 19-23, **20, 21**
exoskeleton, 26
eyes, 29-30, **30,** 55

family trees, **16-17, 90-91**
fangs, 25, 38-39, 40

food, 28, 44, 50, 66, 83
fossils, **18,** 19-23, **20, 21,
      23,** 24

legs, 25-26
life cycle, 75-81
lifespan, 75

hair, 30-31, **31,** 36, **36**
harvestman, **11, 52,** 65-
      66, **65,** 67, **67,** 75
humans, 81-85

Megarachne, 24
mesothelids, 34-35
mite, **11,** 24, 46, **52,** 66-71,
      68, 69, 70, 77, 77,
      81-82
      chigger, 68-69, **68**
      dust, 70, **70**
      red spider, 69, **69**
molt, 77, 79
mygalomorph, 35-39 **35,
      36, 37**

Oonopidae, 43
orb weavers, 44, 47
oviparous, 79
      See also eggs

palps, 25, 29, 54

parthenogenesis, 79
pectines, 55-56
pedipalps *See* palps
Pholcidae, 43, 67, **67**
Pisauridae, 42
pseudoscorpion, 57-58, **57**

reproduction, 25, 51, **51,**
      56, 73, **74,** 75-81,
      76, 77, 78

Salticidae, 43
scorpion, 15, 53-57
      body structure, 54-57,
      55
      emperor, **56**
      as food, 83-84, **83**
      habitat, 53-54
      microwhip, 15, 60
      reproduction, 78-79,
      80, **80**
      sting, 57
      tail, 54-55,
      whip, 26, 58-59, **59**
senses, 29-30, 55-56
silk, 35, 46-51
solifugid, 63-65
spider, 12, 13, 15, 22, **23,**
      24, 33-51
      black widow, 14, 76,
      76

body structure, 23-27, **25,**
crab, **6,** 44-46, **44, 45,** 77, 84, 84
deadliest, 38, **39**
endangered, 86-87, **87**
fishing, 42-43, **42**
funnel-web, 36, 37-38, **38, 39**
    Sydney, 37-38, **39**
Goliath bird-eating, 24
habitat, 33-34, 37-39, 43
hooded tick, 61-62, **61**
huntsman, 42
interior anatomy, **28**

jumping, 41, 41, 43, **43**
Kauai cave spider, 86-87, **87**
largest, 35-37, **36**
net-casting, 48, 50, **50**
nursery-web, 42
sea, 49, **49**
smallest, 41
sun, 63-65, **64**
trap-door, 38-40, **40**
water, 33, **34**
web, **13,** 46-51, **47, 48**
whip, 26, 62-63, **62**
wolf, **30,** 42
spinnerets, 34, 46
spiracles, 28

stabilimentum, 47, 47
tarantula, 35-37, **35, 36, 37**
taxonomy, 8-15
ticks, 15, 24, 29, **29,** 71-73, **72, 73**
    reproduction, 77-78, **78**

venom, 29, 34, 36, 38, 55, 56
vinegaroon *See* whip scorpion

webs, **13**

ABOUT THE AUTHOR

Rebecca Stefoff is the author of a number of books on scientific subjects for young readers. She has explored the world of plants and animals in Marshall Cavendish's Living Things series and in several volumes of the AnimalWays series, also published by Marshall Cavendish. For the Family Trees series, she has authored books on primates, flowering plants, and more. Stefoff has also written about evolution in *Charles Darwin and the Evolution Revolution* (Oxford University Press, 1996), and she appeared in the *A&E Biography* program on Darwin and his work. Stefoff lives in Portland, Oregon. You can learn more about her and her books at www.rebeccastefoff.com.